ST.HELENS COLLEGE LIBRARY

WITHDRAWN FROM

KT-165-386

093560
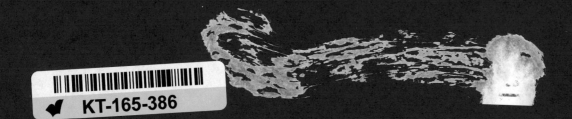

# Old Havana

*Editor*
Alexandre Dórea Ribeiro

*Managing Editor*
Maiá Mendonça

*Editorial project*
Claudio Edinger

*Special consultant*
Pamela Duffy

*DBA Studio coordinator*
Fernando Moser

*Art directors*
Mauricio Nisi Gonçalves
Marcelo Menegolli

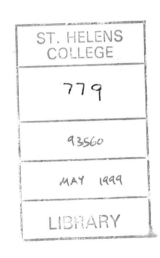
ST. HELENS
COLLEGE

779

93560

MAY 1999

LIBRARY

*Spanish translation (text Guillermo Cabrera Infante)*
Vera Mascarenhas

*English translation*
C. Stuart Birkinshaw

*Producer*
Juliana Ruschel

*Revision*
Touché! Editorial

*Electronic editing*
Shadow Design

*Films and printing*
E.B.S. Verona, Itália

Photographs Copyright © 1998 by Claudio Edinger
Copyright © 1998 by DBA® Dórea Books and Art

*English edition*
Dewi Lewis Publishing
8 Broomfield Road, Heaton Moor, Stockport SK4ND, England
Tel. (0044) 161 442 9450

*German edition*
Edition Stemmle
Alte Landstrasse 55, 8802 Kilchberg, Zurich, Switzerland
Tel. (0041) 01 715 4300

*Distribution in USA*
D.A.P. Distributed Art Publishers
155 Sixth Avenue, New York, N.Y. 10013
Tel. (001) 212 627 1999

All rights reserved. All and any reproduction of this book by any
means or form, be it electronic or mechanical, photocopy, recording
or other means of reproduction is prohibited without the express
permission of the publishers.

# Old Havana

Photographs by Claudio Edinger

Texts by Guillermo Cabrera Infante and Humberto Werneck

DEWI LEWIS
PUBLISHING

4

# Acknowledgements

To Alexandre Dórea Ribeiro, our Brazilian publisher, for his rare sensibility. To G. Cabrera Infante for the book's introduction and Humberto Werneck for his marvellous text. To our English publisher Dewi Lewis for being such a great man, and to Dr. Thomas Stemmle our German publisher.

To Augusto de Carvalho Alves, Alberto de Carvalho Alves, Renato Ganhito, Luis Carlos Scholz, Fabio Starace Fonseca, Zélio Alves Pinto, Marcos Mendonça, Fábio Magalhães, Carlos Alberto Dêgelo, for their sensibility and generosity, making this book possible.

To Dascha Edinger, Christina Cunali, Juliana Ruschel, João Farkas, Fátima Leão, Maria Emilia de Queiroz Telles Cunali, Carlos Carvalhosa, Zita Carvalhosa, Jay Colton, Pamela Duffy, Thomas Csiha, Cathy Colon, Gene, Thomaz Farkas, Flávio Bitelman, Claudio Vasconcelos, Kleuber Pereira, Carlos Peres, Fabíola Chiminazzo, Isabel Amado, Ruth Sporn, Thomas Gutierrez Alea (in memoriam), Mirtha Ibarra, Arthur Nestrovski, Ana Luiza Arditti, Rob Stevens, Dorrit Harazim, Sharon Gallagher, Avery Lozada, Didier Kelly, Marcel Saba, Phil Block, Ed Rich, Joan Menschenfreund and Elias Landsberg, for their friendship, advice, patience, support, and faith in this project.

To Maiá Mendonça, Adriana Amback, Fernando Moser, Marcelo Menegolli, Mauricio Nisi Gonçalves, Linda Vilas Boas, Carmen S. de Carvalho, Sílvia Ghirello, Maria do Socorro Sabóia and Bob Lima, all part of DBA's team who made this book possible.

Without the generous sponsorship of Enterpa, Social Cheque, and financial support of Friozem, Secretaria de Cultura do Estado de São Paulo, Memorial da America Latina and Centro Cultural Banco do Brasil, this book would not have happened.

This book was photographed with Mamiya 6 cameras, flash Vivitar 285 HV and Fuji Próvia film. All the film was processed and the prints were made at Aurora Color Lab in New York.

I am especially grateful to Paramahansa Yogananda.

6

To Christina

# Havana as a metaphor

by Guillermo Cabrera Infante

A metaphor is an "implied comparison". The metaphor is a basic figure of speech and usually is associated with a myth. In this sense, Cuba's metaphor is Havana, which in turn is the embodiment of a myth – if indeed a city can be an embodiment of something. For me, Havana is not just the metaphor of Cuba (Havana is the very soul of Cuba), but also the source of my dreams – and of my nightmares. The Havana of my dreams is a city evoked out of nostalgia. The Havana of today is a source of nightmares: incubus and succubus at once. There is no more to be seen except for the streets that seem to be dying, perishing under the cruel internal bombardment: only ruins are left, and although as Horace said, "Ruins will find me undaunted", these ruins leave me moved, dismayed and at the same time intrigued.

One cannot compare Havana with Rome or Athens, the amphorae of beautiful ruins, which the photographers of today's Havana insist on showing to the contrary. Claudio Edinger is one of those insistent photographers that awaken our graphic senses to the beauty existing in Havana. It is not a continuous image of the aesthetics of misery, but an ethic that insists on being profoundly moral. Your Havana is not mine: yours is current, mine is intellectual and therefore visible only as long as memory lasts. However my memories are not enough: I want to return to Havana before I die. Meanwhile, I leaf through photographs looking for something in common, and Edinger seems to have found it. Without references however, as the eye enjoys what the soul cannot see.

# Cuba today:
# Happy go lucky creativity

by Humberto Werneck

You have just rented a car in the suburb of El Vedado, in Havana, and have not even driven half a block when you see the young man on the sidewalk of Calle 21 trying to say something: ...*?Kilometraje? ?Kilometraje?*

Even not speaking Spanish, you would wind up understanding what he wants, behind the skinny, vaguely guevaristic mustache of so many young Cubans: for 10 dollars, and not a cent more, he will fix the car so that the odometer does not register more than 100 kilometers per day. A great saving, *?verdad?* argues the lad, reminding one that the state agency, Havanautos, charges 30 cents for any additional kilometers. Another 34 kilometers, and the investment will have paid for itself, he states, to the surprise of someone not expecting such an ardent salesman in a communist country. We understand perfectly but we're not interested, *gracias*. The thin mustache does not give up so easily: how about cigars? A bottle of rum?

A few little boxes of PPG?... And he launches into a dissertation on the prodigious effects of this exclusively Cuban drug which reduces your cholesterol level and, even more sensational, enhances your sexual vigor. If you close a sale, the ingratiating kilometer stretcher will take a quick trip over there to fetch the merchandise. If you do not go along with his spiel he will keep on insisting, and eventually ask whether the friend has in his hotel a spare *pulover* (T-shirt) he doesn't need? Because, *señor* understands, *no es fácil* (life isn't easy).

One just has to note the frequency with which the three words *no es facil* are heard in Cuban's conversations. They should be on one of those billboards, now somewhat rusty, with which the Castro regime tries to keep alive the enthusiasm of its people and which lately have begun to make room for other advertisements, like the brand new one for a multinational brand of washing powder that "eliminates dirt and stains". Indeed it is not easy. When in the early 1990's the Soviet Union crumbled, Cuba wound up without the dollars upon which her economy depended (85% of her economy depended on Eastern Europe), and bogged down in a mire pompously baptized as "A Special Period in Time of Peace". The utter penury that this signifies has led Cubans to develop extremes of creativity – there are people raising chickens on their apartment terraces and pigs in their bathrooms – to serve unimaginable dishes such as cat meat or banana-skin steaks, and in many cases to resort to burglary pure and simple as a means of survival. Prostitution, which the Government boasted as having been eliminated, has come back stronger that ever, beneath a general complacency. Without maintenance the houses of Havana, one of the most beautiful cities in the world, are crumbling. Magnificent buildings collapse. And this is not necessarily the end: Fidel, who blamed all the present troubles on the trade restrictions imposed by the United States since the early 1960's, has already raised the theory of a frightening "Option Zero", whereby, without a drop of oil left – which fuels all the island's energy –

people will have to live in the fields and work the land. As there will also be no food, this will have to be a colossal *caldoza*, a traditional poor-man's soup.

The Cubans' table, never excessively plentiful, became even scarcer: of the 400 daily grams of food guaranteed by the *libreta*, the basic food ration subsidized by the State, only 27 are foodstuffs rich in protein – the reason why cases are increasing of diseases caused by malnutrition. With no oil, buses and cars are being laid up, replaced by bicycles, just as on the fields they have returned to the plough, as over 80,000 tractors are stopped for lack of diesel oil. For several years the country was steeped in darkness, with the routine of the *apagones*, the prolonged and not always predictable electric power cuts which often caused the loss of the little that had been left in refrigerators.

Even the conquests of which the Socialist revolution are so proud, the education and health systems, are also at risk. The island lacks over 400 brands of medicines, from antibiotics to simple physiological serum. Work centers have closed down by the hundreds and the workers in jobs have had their wages reduced. Cuban money is worthless. The highest salaries in the country, of a veterinary for example, of around 400 pesos, in March 1994 was equal to no more than 4 dollars – not enough to purchase one-and-a-half chickens on Havana's black market.

Since then the situation has improved considerably. Three years after the 1993 slump, Cuba's economy grew 7.6% in 1996. Four hundred pesos are now worth 20 Dollars. Even so, *no es facil* – and that is why the young lad with the mustache is there, on the sidewalk of Calle 21, offering his services to falsify odometers. At night he will probably be out offering his own body, preferably on the corners of Hotel Habana Libre, the Yara cinema and Coppelia ice-cream parlor, a busy crossroads at the top of the *Rampa*, as the section is known that leads down toward the sea. That is where the majority of the *jineteros* and *jineteras* hang out (in a literal sense, he or she who mounts a *ginete*, or a spirited steed), all of them *luchando un yuma*, for affairs that may each yield from 20 to 100 *fulas*, as the dollar is also called. Under the worst of circumstances, the equivalent of the highest salary paid in Cuba.

Many people, and not just the *jineteros* now live off *trampas*, swindles, in this land that, in the definition of a native, is small but problematic. For *no es facil*. Gasoline that may be bought for 50 cents on the black market costs almost half that which is sold at filling stations at 90 cents, but it may contain a large amount of water. Buying a *tableta de mani*, a peanut sweetmeat sold in the streets for 5 pesos, you run the risk of chewing on beans mixed with the peanuts. In the queues in front of stores, in front of the United States Interests Office, there will certainly be more than one citizen not interested in buying or in emigrating, but rather in selling, for 5 dollars, his place in the lethargic human serpent. The people who get up at dawn to purchase a copy of *Granma* are not merely interested in reading the fastidious journal of the Communist Party: they will buy it for 20 *kilos* (20 cents) and then resell it as soon as the copies run out, for 1 peso. And it is likely that the buyer of this second-hand *Granma* is less interested in the news than in its use as a replacement for the toilet paper no longer available in stores.

Anyone knows that it is possible to adjust the water meter and the electricity meter so as to pay less. There are also many who borrow household appliances from friends and neighbors on the day the inspector is to visit, as the consumption allowed for each consumer depends upon the number of appliances he has in his home. A while back, the inexhaustible resourcefulness of the Cuban imagination invented a means of avoiding the *apagones*:

one simply rigged a *tendedera*, or an extension wire from one house to another situated close by but in an area where the power cuts occurred at a different time. The *tendedera* meant that neither of the houses went without electricity. In the suburb of Miramar, a traditional redoubt of the well-to-do of Havana, extension cables such as these extend for blocks around.

"The *apagones* used to hurt more than the lack of food", a housewife recalls in Cojímar, a seaside city 15 kilometers away from the capital, fearful that the nightmare might return. The power cuts which according to a resident in Havana transformed the city into a Christmas tree, would cut out here, come back there, radically changing the life of Cubans. People avoided staying at home during night time *apagones*, arranging visits for these periods. And many times these calls were also abruptly terminated, as within minutes there was no longer an elevator.

The lack of public lighting caused an increase in crimes, such as bicycle robberies, sometimes including violence and deaths. The majority of cinemas had their screenings reduced to one session, and only on Thursdays, Saturdays and Sundays. The Coppelia ice-cream parlor, a popular resort for many, which would close at 1:45 am, had to close at 8 pm. Transmissions of the two TV channels, Cubavisión and Telerebelde were also shortened, from 6 to 11 pm, 24 hours maximum, allowed to operate till 1 in the morning on Saturdays. In the Summer of 1993, when the last chapter of the Brazilian soap opera *Vale Tudo* was to go on the air there was an *apagon* in Bauta, 23 kilometers from Havana. The people took to the streets, shouting and yelling – until the lights came on again.

During that same torrid Summer, when power cuts could last as much as eight hours, there were a series of incidents in Havana, with the population breaking bottles in the darkened streets, as, unable to use their air conditioners, it was impossible to sleep. In the suburb of El Cerro, there were so many hold-ups in *bodegas* (bars) that the authorities decided that there would be no further power cuts in that area. It certainly is a tough place. Not so long ago eleven steers on the way to the slaughterhouse disappeared, simply vanished from the streets without leaving any trace, steaks, horns or even a bellow. The driver of the truck transporting them does not know what happened.

The shortages introduced a new way of life, one of wartime, in which swindles and more are acceptable. "This was given me by Roberto", you would hear with a malicious smile, and it was not hard to perceive that the generous Roberto is an imaginary individual whose name derives from the word *robo* (stolen). From whence came the box of 25 Cohiba *lanceros* (Fidel's cigar until he gave up the habit in 1985) which the lad in Calle 21 offers to tourists for 20 or 25 dollars, when the price in the stores is 264? Or the box of PPG, which dropped in price from 20 dollars to 3? Where did the articles come from on sale in the *bolsa negra* (black market) where one comes across absolutely everything no longer available in State stores, and much more?

The fact is that without a store of "greenbacks" it is practically impossible to survive in Cuba, so when the Government authorized the ownership of foreign exchange in July, 1993, there was a run on the *fula*. (Ironically there are still people in prison for having been caught with dollars before this). What to do, if all salaries are in pesos? Improvise. There are those who offer to tourists, for 1 or 2 dollars, bank notes and coins of 3 pesos with the picture of Che Guevara – he of all people, the proclaimer of the *hombre nuevo* (new man) who disdained any type of material incentive. *Jineteros* and *jineteras* latch onto foreigners, ignoring the prohibition of going up with them to their hotel rooms. (No Cuban can register at the better hotels, even if he has a pocket full of *fulas*, as under a pretext of protecting visitors a virtual touristic apartheid is in force in the country). Judging by the remarks of one of these girls, there is no problem that Abraham Lincoln – whose face adorns 5 dollar notes – cannot solve, as long as doormen, elevator operators and room servants remain understanding. Alternatively, other citizens have begun to rent rooms or houses to foreigners, which is illegal. A house for 20 dollars a day is not hard to find. In the suburb of Vedado, a room with a bathroom, for one night, is worth 10 dollars – which for many tourists looking for sex is a good alternative, considering the prohibition of taking Cubans to a hotel and the decrepitude of *posadas*, motels at the doors of which in other days, impatient lines of couples would be waiting.

But there are other sources of *fulas* besides prostitution, street-corner salesmanship and under-the-table rentals. "Just as well that I have *fé* (faith)", some of the luckier ones say,

14

with the magnificent if inexplicable good humor of the Cubans. Fé (faith) in this case are the initials for "familia no exterior" (family abroad). Those with family members in the United States – where over 1 million Cubanos live, as against 10.7 million living on the island – are allowed up to 300 dollars every three months, a limit imposed by the American Government. Illegally, a volume of cash impossible to calculate enters the country in the baggage of exiles visiting their families (there are flights between Cuba and Florida via Mexico), or on the backs of *caballos*, smugglers of money working the Miami-Havana circuit. People will do anything to send help to family members on the island. There is a story about the unfortunate Cuban who asked his brother in Florida for help and was disappointed when he received no more than a pair of shoes, one size too small at that. He sold them to a stranger, and then nearly went mad when he later discovered that the ingenious brother had hidden 1,000 dollars in each shoe.

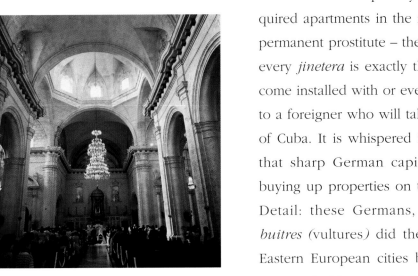

Paseo de Martí, armed with little books you may peruse upon payment of 5 pesos, or for the same price put in your own offer. Properties located in areas where there are no *apagones* – close to hotels or hospitals, for example – are highly valued and the ads hasten to mention these features. The barter of properties of different values almost always signifies that some cash has passed between the interested parties. In the case of Cubanos in Miami, who have nothing to barter, the purchase is made in the name of some family member. Foreign businessmen who visit Havana frequently have acquired apartments in the name of a permanent prostitute – the dream of every *jinetera* is exactly this, to become installed with or even married to a foreigner who will take her out of Cuba. It is whispered in Havana that sharp German capitalists are buying up properties on the island. Detail: these Germans, veritable *buitres* (vultures) did the same in Eastern European cities before the communist bloc crumbled.

15

Some of the money coming from Miami has been invested in houses and apartments belonging to private individuals. One solemnly ignores the law prohibiting the sale or purchase of real estate in Cuba – while prices increase: a house that could have been purchased last year for 15,000 dollars today is worth 50,000. The *trampa* in this case consists of presenting these transactions as barter, which is perfectly legal. So there has sprung up a "barter agent" – sometimes working in the open, as under the trees in the

The Cubans don't trade just real estate. Everything is being bartered all the time and in these transactions equivalents are established which no one questions. One good sized hog equals one bicycle. In the country, one bar of toilet soap is worth thirty eggs, a bar of laundry soap is exchanged for two pounds of coffee, five of rice, four of beans or three bottles of tomato sauce. There have been cases of a sheep being exchanged for a food blender, while a washing machine has been traded for a pair of blue jeans. The crisis at least had the merit of awakening in the Cubanos an entrepreneurial appetite believed to have been dulled by three and a half decades of State management. It gave new blood to a well-known figure the *bisnero*, one who is involved in *bisne* (a businessman). There are those who travel out into the country and come back with sacks of merchandise to sell at a handsome profit in the city. The same box containing thirty eggs the farmer sold for 1 dollar will be resold for 3.

In September, 1993, the Government authorized free-lance operations in 117 lines of activity, among them that of "producer of fast foods", which was enough for a rash, in Havana and in the seaside resort of Varadero, 140 kilometers away from the capital, of dozens or even hundreds of domestic restaurants, all keen for the tourist's dollars. They were glorified versions of the traditional *tiros clandestinos*, the illegal operation, although tolerated, of food and drink sold in homes. Charging no more than 5 dollars for lunches and dinners that in state-owned establishments would cost fifteen or twenty times as much, the success was immediate. Like the restaurant of the character Raquel, played by Brazilian actress Regina Duarte in the TV soap opera *Vale Tudo* which Cubans followed avidly, these domestic restaurants became popular under the name *paladar*. Some of these, slightly more costly, reached a surprising degree of sophistication, with lobster on the menu (80 cents each, or 4 dollars a kilo on Havana's black market), imported beer, reservations re-

quired, television, live music, clandestine taxi services, and to leave no doubt that you are still in Cuba, a waiting line outside the door. Many of these *paladares* were operated by actors and actresses, who besides earning a few extra dollars, rediscovered the pleasure of playing the host, no longer possible due to scarcity well before the "special period". Tourists would be discreetly approached – *¿Comida? ¿Comida?* – on the streets of Havana and Varadero. "Note that no one opens a picture gallery or something similar" observes one of Havana's plastic artists. "People know that the important thing is food".

Everything was going along nicely until in December of the same year the Government decide to outlaw the *paladares*, claiming that they were selling food stolen or side-tracked from the state network – which was true. Practically all the raw materials were purchased from people who make a living from traveling into the countryside to forage for food. A risky activity, as the police are liable to arrest and fine anyone caught with excessive quantities of eggs, sugar, salt, coffee, beef and horse meat. But the prohibition did not manage to completely close down the *paladares*. In one of the best suburbs of Havana one of them defied the law with a red awning, red lighting, swinging doors and even advertising for Heineken beer. Others, less audacious, would deliver meals to your home, with a minimum of 4 meals at 1 dollar each. And there was at least one phone-a-pizza service with the oven alight in Havana. "You don't learn capitalism" states the same artist, "it springs up from inside you". What is seen today is not yet capitalism but rather a hybrid system which has been called *"capi-socialism"*, with a bustling underground market economy handling dollars the State hasn't managed to lay its hands on. In an attempt to capture at least part of this money the Government has recently relented and freed the *paladares*, which may now be operated openly, paying taxes, as in a capitalist economy.

With so many work centers deactivated or working at half strength, thousands of Cubanos see no way out other than to fight for themselves. From the entrails of the State there have sprung up active carpenters, bricklayers, make-up artists, massagists, photographers, watch menders, animal trainers, baby sitters, domestic servants and even magicians and clowns, under the heading "animators of childrens' parties". In a short time the population real-

ized that private operators were offering better quality than state ones, keen as they are to prosper, contrary to what happens at the immense and lethargic counters of the Cuban public service. To cite just two examples, hairdressers and manicurists (professions which already had been liberated) work with fine articles brought in from Miami by family members or purchased in dollars at the *diplotiendas*, shops that for many years had been exclusively for foreigners – while on the public network they ask customers to bring their own products from home. "Please bring your

own towel" was seen recently in the window of *Peluqueria Ensueño*, in Calle Obispo, also informing as if offering a great privilege: "We have shampoo".

The possibility of working for themselves has awakened the Cubans' creativity – for which they are unusually apt, in fact there is in the country a National Association of Innovators and Rationalizers, with no less than 300,000 members. So that it is not surprising that Cuba is probably the only country in the world where there are people restoring discardable cigarette lighters. As the cheapest *fosforera* costs 75 cents of a dollar in the stores, on the sidewalks there is a proliferation of stalls where you can recharge it or change the flint for 2 pesos. To the dismay of tourists, the gas often comes in recycled tubes of insecticide spray.

17

In Cuba everything is recycled. The tube of a fluorescent lamp, cut short and mounted on a medicine bottle filled with *luz brillante* (kerozene) becomes an attractive little oil lamp. Cigarette and cigar buts may be converted into *tupamaros*, hand-crafted cigarettes put in style by another tobacco shortage such as that of the 1970's and reborn as soon as the libreta does not guarantee to every citizen more than four cigars and six packs of cigarettes per month. The apparatus for making *tupamaros* is a rustic and oversized brother of the one used in capitalist countries to roll joints. It produces a long cigarette that has to be cut in half. The paper is that used for tracing maps in school books.

Old Russian television sets with burned-out picture tubes return to service fitted with (also Russian) computer monitor screens, for which one pays 71 pesos. The original picture tubes ran out along with the Soviet Union, but there are lots of monitor screens – without their respective computers, which did not arrive in time. As the monitor screen is much smaller than the original, one has to adapt a frame of plywood or cardboard. But there's nothing that can be done about the inevitable green coloring of Moscow's prehistoric computers.

For quite a long time, at the beginning of the Special Period, the roofs of Havana were cluttered with improvised parabolic antennas, *parábolas.* They all pointed to the tower on the Haban Libre hotel, which, linked to a satellite, redistributed to the other hotels the images from a dozen or so US and Mexican stations. It was not always easy to install these contraptions. In downtown Calle San Lázaro, cables and antennas reached out as far as the center of the street, or else climbed up to where they could see the hotel. Small, usually less than one meter in diameter, the *parábolas* cost 150 dollars and were made of aluminum, often gleaned from plates removed from off-set printing machines, or made simply of wire netting. The electronic components came from Miami, where a complete kit cost 35 dollars. The Cubans discovered that the best way to fit it to the antenna was to use an empty sun-flower oil can, a donation from the Italian Government. For a channel

selector, some had the idea of installing it in a telephone set, where you would dial to tune in your station.

For a while the Government turned a blind eye on the *parábolas* festival, as if to admit that TV was one of the few amusements available to the people. But then the precarious antennas began to disappear from the skies of Havana, as the State suddenly decided to code the TV signals. As in any country, you now only receive an image if you pay for a decoder.

At the height of the *parábolas* fashion, Cuban spectators discovered the marvels of US broadcasting, especially the advertising. They would say "Ah, so that's what a Big Mac is..." Until shortages had really become serious, there had been a few snack bars, which the Havana population called "McDonalds", in which one could eat a hamburger sandwich named either a "MacCastro", or in an allusion to the American Burger King fast food chain and to the *comandante's* trade mark, a "Barber King".

It is probably on the subject of food that the Cubano's creativity has most come into play during this "special period". With the lack of *bijol*, a yellow powder used to color foods, housewives came up with the idea of cooking their rice with vitamin B tablets that the Government distributes to prevent malnutrition (and which unfortunately has the effect of increasing the appetite). "The flavor is the same" one of them says. Nearly all of them have resorted to a trick much used during the 1980's, which consists of placing three or four marbles with the ground coffee in an Italian type coffee maker: it increases the pressure they claim, and you use less coffee, which always comes mixed with something – either wheat or the small green-gray grains of the chick-pea. This is no invention of Socialism, even before the end of the revolution, in early 1959, the capitalist coffee used to come with ground chick-pea.

The shortage has taught Cubans how to make mayonnaise with almost no eggs. "Almost no cholesterol" an enthusiastic youngster claims of this emergency mayonnaise, and provides the recipe: two or three boiled potatoes beaten in the food blender with vinegar, salt, garlic, a little oil and only one egg. Homemade wines are made out of all types of fruit - grapefruit, sugarcane, pineapple, coconut, beet root, rice, chick-pea and even grapes. Cubans also make *azuquín*, a brandy distilled from sugar or molasses, to drink when they run out of the low quality rum included in the *libreta*: no more than half a liter per month per family, no matter of what size. And this half liter is called a *sábado corto* – an allusion to the Saturdays when, before the "special period", one did not work. Today no one works on any Saturdays.

Beef, the obsessive dream of everyone has found unexpected substitutes in Cuba, where one same dish permits a diner to be both a meat-eater and a vegetarian at the same

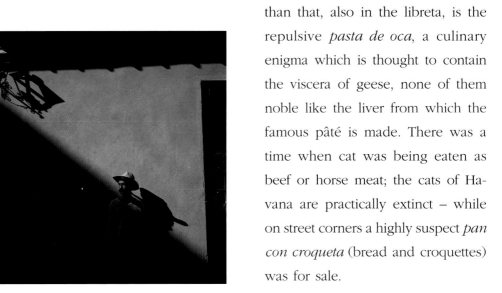

time: slices of grapefruit artfully seasoned and fried result in a grapefruit steak. The same is done with the skins of plantains and with *gofio* (roasted and ground wheat). "We are discovering that beef has no flavor", one Cuban states jovially, "as everything can have the flavor of meat". Everything, that is, except for the *picadillo* of the libreta, comprised of second grade ground meat mixed with soybean. In the jargon of the bureaucrat – capable of prodigious feats of rhetoric such as a "meatsome mass" – this is the *picadillo extendido*, which does nothing to render it palatable. Worse than that, also in the libreta, is the repulsive *pasta de oca*, a culinary enigma which is thought to contain the viscera of geese, none of them noble like the liver from which the famous pâté is made. There was a time when cat was being eaten as beef or horse meat; the cats of Havana are practically extinct – while on street corners a highly suspect *pan con croqueta* (bread and croquettes) was for sale.

The city's pigs and chickens were more fortunate, as they are valuable on the black market, and are reared in the homes – that is *inside* the homes. Often on the second or third floor of an apartment building. Daybreak in downtown Havana reminds one of a chicken farm, what with the crowing emanating from the buildings. Havana is the only city in the world where pigs do not live up to their reputation: they are spotlessly clean, as they mingle with their owners, and are confined in a bathroom or a verandah, sometimes spending the night in the living room. The Cuban film *Fresa y Chocolate*

(Strawberries and Chocolate) showed to the world the comic spectacle of a pig being pushed up the stairs by the residents in a tenement. So as to avoid attracting attention, as raising pigs in the home is not allowed – swine fever caused a great deal of damage in the 1970's and '80's – there are those who have the animal's vocal chords cut, a practice so wide-spread that it is mentioned in another film *Adorable Lies*. Pigs are mute. Others feed the pigs pills to make them sleep all day, though the pork loses its quality and their bones are weak. For this reason the pigs of Havana do not fetch high prices on the black market.

Deodorants are made at home from sodium bicarbonate, as is soap, made from caustic soda and mutton or pork fat, which also in extreme cases has been used as toothpaste. There is not much to be done to remedy the shortage of feminine sanitary absorbents which the libreta theoretically ensures but which arrive in insufficient quantities – eight per month – and at intervals to outshine

even the most irregular menstrual cycles. "Last year they were handed out in January and again only in September" bemoans the mother of a family, with the *libreta* in hand. As a box of eight Tampax costs 6.80 dollars on the black market, they have returned to the antiquated and vexatious napkins, and some women simply refuse to leave their homes on those days.

The Cubans' imaginations were stretched even further to face the breakdown in the transport system, one of the

sectors where life is even harder. If before the "special period" it already was not easy to catch a bus, today it is a torment. Crowds jostle one another on the pavements at bus stops. Public workers dressed in egg-yellow uniforms and therefore dubbed *amarillos*, stop state cars in the streets to accommodate passengers. The *amarillo* feature in a joke going around Havana in the first days of the crisis, the *cuento de los colores* (story of the colors) illustrative of the tormentuous day-to-day living of a Cuban: you wake up *en blanco* (white, that is fasting), go out to *luchar un verde* (fight for a dollar, or greenback), look for an *amarillo;* if you are going by car or bicycle, take care to not be stopped by a *cinza* (gray, a traffic warden), or even worse by *un azul* (blue, a policeman); and then go to bed *en negro* (in the dark of an *apagón*).

To beg a ride has become routine. Many walk for kilometers. Whoever can afford it buys a bicycle, usually imported from China or East Europe, which in the streets competes with the heavy, hard, almost ergometric Cuban bicycles. It also competes with the *Tren Bus*, an enormous bus mounted on the chassis of a truck, for 200 passengers, with two humps in the body which earned it the nickname of a *camello*. Also due to the imagination of the bureaucrat is the *Ciclo Bus*, for transporting bicycles through the tunnel between Havana and its eastern zone, and the bizarre *ladalimusina*, resulting from stretching the tiny Lada automobile. With its tiny wheels and its raised rear end, giving the alarming impression that it's about to break in half at any moment, this automobilistic frankenstein does not even remotely aspire to the charm of its New York counterpart – it just wants to be a taxi for more people.

There are state taxis, such as these *ladalimusinas* and the Japanese cars of the Turistaxi fleet, but there are also private cars (250,000 cars, half of the motorized vehicles existing in Cuba do not belong to the State), and many of them are clandestine. Nothing of course identifies them as taxis, but they circulate freely and each one brings in from 20 to 30 dollars a day. The problem is the gasoline. The libreta gives you the right to buy 20 liters a month, for which you pay 5.80 pesos. But reality is somewhat different. During the first eleven months of last year no more than 60 liters were distributed per car. The answer is to resort, with dollars, to gas stations or the black market. With private taxis each trip has its price negotiated previously, and like so many other things in Cuba, a foreigner winds up paying more. A trip to Varadero, one way, costs 86.50 dollars in a Turistaxi; in a private taxi a foreigner may make the trip for 20, while a Cubano could pay 3.

In Cuba there are bicycles circulating with engines taken from fumigators and even chain saws. There are also bicycle by-products such as the *bicitaxi*, which offers

passengers the comfort of a roof, and the *bicicoche*, a small four-wheeled vehicle able to transport a family. None of them however are more ingenious than the *bicipalma*, invented by one Pablo Morales Echarte. It weighs 34 kilos and is used to climb a coconut palm and pick the nuts. (It is said in Cuba that the Japanese already have an eye on the contraption). Pablo Morales could become a popular hero if he were to now invent a bicycle that climbs stairs, as everyone has to store their bike indoors, even if this means a third floor apartment with no elevator, because of thieves. Havana already has bicycle guards, charging 2 pesos, as well as car guards who expect tourists to pay them *un kilito*, any currency with a value of one dollar – even a "cash certificate", notes and coins circulated by the State and equivalent to US money. The car washer is another novelty in Havana. One of them is an administration technician who leaves his job, picks up his can, rags and soap and washes the cars in a hotel. On a bad day he will return home with the equivalent of 25 pesos – a tenth part of his monthly salary.

The list of new occupations in Cuba includes street vendors of all sorts of things – from faucets to vases of recycled plastic, through to used disks and books. Citizens who wish to sell something do not always advertise; one stands at one's street door with the merchandise in hand – a chicken, say – in silence, so as not to call the attention of some *chivato*, a finger-man of the CDR, the still active Committee for the Defense of the Revolution, or, worse, the truculent Quick Response Brigades, the watchdogs of the regime. Streets at several spots of Havana have become known as *Calle Ocho* – the famous 8th Street of Miami, where Cuban exiles established their places of business during the first years of exile. At first sight the *calles ocho* of Havana are merely homes, but announcements by word of mouth inform that several houses function as veritable shops.

For some time legal commerce has included *casas comisionistas*, on whose shelves anybody may place on consignment whatever he or she wishes to sell, pocketing a commission of from 85% to 30%, depending upon the time taken to sell it. In one of them, in the Boulevard in downtown Havana, under a tropical heat, there is no lack of fur coats which were probably intended for Moscow but which the collapse of the socialist bloc have left with no traveling in sight. Until recently people had been placing articles on sale in conventional stores working with dollars, with the collusion of the shop workers, but the State put a stop to this game.

The Cuban shops where the peso is the currency are pathetic. One feels like leaving one's watch or camera there. El Trianon, in the city center, that during the days of capitalism sold jewelry and art objects, today

displays ordinary plastic articles, a situation they try to ease by offering customers water to drink or free telephone services. The little that is sold in stores of this type are things no one wants – over-size Bulgarian shoes, for example, or *guayaberas* (large shirts typical of the Caribbean) in aggressively synthetic fabrics. No one wants these horrors, especially now that Cubans have been allowed to buy in the dollar stores. Many people resentfully state that the Government puts on sale in these *diplotiendas* foodstuffs received from other countries as donations. This may be no more than hearsay, such as the story that *el comandante* likes to sleep under a baric chamber, like Michael Jackson. What is certain is that once powdered milk donated by Spain appeared on the shelves. There was a great scandal, and the Government explained that the sale of the product, in dollars, would enable the purchase of twice as much milk.

Unlike the tourists, the native Cubans, even armed with dollars, have to queue in the stores. Not so long ago, in a *diplotienda*, Cubans protested when a countrywoman, exiled in Miami (the State authorizes quick visits to the island "for humanitarian reasons" – a death in the family, a sick father) wanted to bypass the queue. The manager appeared and explained the marvels of a new approach to the exiles. "It's not fair that this lady, who has come to Cuba to see her family, spends time in a queue", he argued. "After all, most of you receive your money from people like this lady, who with loving sacrifice send you what they can". He was almost applauded.

But times, in fact, are different, and ironically the privileged few are exactly the same as those who do not agree with the regime and have gone to live in Miami – except of course the pampered foreign tourist, a kind of floating bourgeoisie in a country that has chased its own away. They are ever more numerous. In 1996, roughly 1.8 million Italians, Canadians, Spaniards, Germans, French, Mexicans, English and Colombians, in that order, visited Fidel's island, where tourism today is the major source of income, ahead of sugar, having left behind 1,3 billion dollars.

They no longer call exiles *gusano* (worm) as they did at the beginning of the revolution, when a poem by Pablo Neruda about the Porto Rico tyrant Muñoz Marín (*"hay un gordo gusano en estas aguas..."*) added the insult to the leftist glossary. Some call these wealthy brethren *mariposas* (butterflies) as the offspring of larvae. Those who had been *gusanos*, became *la comunidad*, and are now *cubanos en el exterior* (Cubans abroad). At this rate, they laugh on the island, they will soon be called *queridos compañeros cubanos en el exterior* (dear Cuban comrades abroad).

The problem is that the term *compañero* is somewhat out of fashion. It is used less and less, leaving more room for the older bourgeois form of address *señor*. Also out of fashion is the ideological tourism of less special periods – although there are still those who visit Havana as if conducting a political safari in a reserve of exotic ideologies, usually Latin Americans homesick for the socialism they never had and which, they suspect, they are not going to get. Today the tourist is less interested in the Museum of the Revolution than in the stupendous state *mulatas* of the Tropicana, or in the French temptations that are whispered at the exit of the legendary cabaret: a *tableau vivant*, no less than explicit sex right under the nose of Fidel.

In comes *señor*, out goes *compañero* – but no one knows what's coming next in Cuba. "Everything will depend upon the peoples' sentiments in relation to *him*", says a local writer, "and in the bottom of their hearts the Cubans have still not decided whether they want him or not". Not so long ago on a street corner in downtown Havana a citizen was shouting out to all and sundry *"!Yo voy a ver quien pinga va a votar por este singao!"* – minus the two swear words, "I want to see who's going to vote for this guy". The people around appeared to be shocked, but only at the swear words. An outsider might not have known who the citizen was talking about – to swear or criticize an unimaginable practice in Cuba for a long time yet today to be found all over the island – they never mention the *comandante*. It is *El Tio, El Papá, El quien tu sabes* (Uncle, Big Daddy, You-know-who), or "banana-stain" as it is green and unremovable. There are those who replace the name with a gesture of the hand stroking an imaginary beard. The leaders in general are referred to more openly: *"Comuní, comuní / to'pa'ti, / na'pa'mi"* (Communist, communist, all for you, nothing for me) is heard from many a Cuban, always slurring his words. The general feeling is of tiredness, irritation, but not despair. Except for those who, with no strength left, merely await the *caldoza*, the great multiple soup that Fidel has promised to serve when the tragic "Option Zero" arrives, to dispatch everyone to the fields. It hasn't gone that far, but already it is not easy.

24

26

28

30

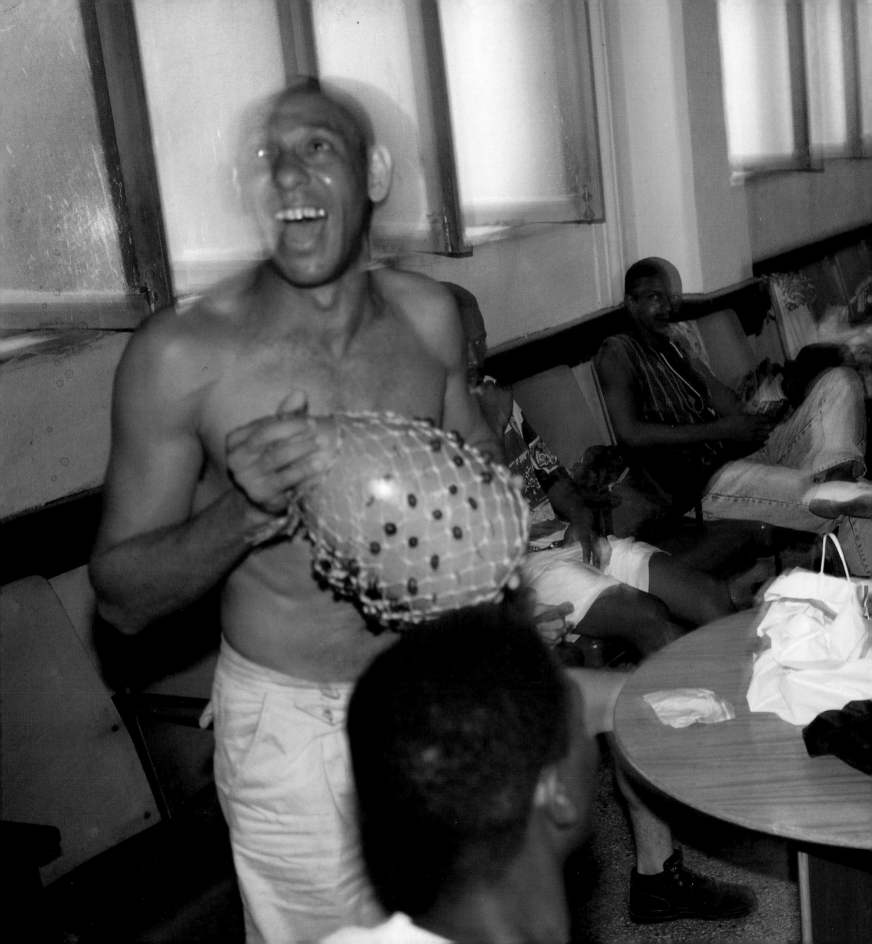

38

42

48

54

58

68

74

90

96

102

106

112

118

128

134

# Captions

9

The Parque Central is the most attractive park in the city. A meeting point for *habaneros*, for the sale of cigars and black market dollars.

13

Cito Assahari, 66, eight children from three different women. Neither he nor his children - a pilot, a chief of police and a veterinarian - have ever left Cuba. He is the janitor of the building he lives in and raises over twenty agoutis. "They are tastier than suckling pig" he claims.

3

Israel Varone, 40, married, 3 children. A sculptor, he carves female figures and sells them to visitors in the seaside city of Varadero, one of the main tourist centers of the island.

11

The terrace of Hotel Inglaterra, the oldest in the capital. With its colonial architecture and Spanish style, it was founded in 1875, and is located in front of the Central Plaza and close to the Capitólio.

14

The Virgin Mary is worshipped by Cuban Catholics. The Government's attitude toward religion has changed a lot; in 1998 Cuba receives a visit from Pope John Paul II.

5

Maria Ester Dennis Gomes, 14, works with her father selling pizza pie. She dreams of a debutante party but as her family has no money, her only hope is an aunt who lives in Miami.

12

Pedro Dropeso Martinez, 57, two children. He distributes free water at the traditional "casa del água." Drinking water has always been a problem in the island

15

Masses are crowded every Sunday in Havana's cathedral. Weddings are common, usually financed by family members living in Miami.

16

Ufemio Martinez Gonzales, 72, two sons and three grandchildren. He sells fifty heads of garlic for 40 pesos (roughly 2 dollars). His breakfast is raw garlic with olive oil and bread, which he claims is highly digestive.

19

Julio Mon Pie, 35, bachelor. A construction worker, he helps restore the impoverished, almost abandoned old city.

22

Julio Ramirez, 81, four sons, two grandchildren. Retired, he makes a living making cloth flowers. He sells them in the streets of the city, earning an average of one hundred dollars per month, or five times the highest salary earned by a public attorney.

17

La Bodeguita del Médio, a famous restaurant of Old Havana and an old meeting place used by Ernest Hemingway.

20

Shop window in the center of Old Havana: here they accept Cuban pesos. In Cuba, all trade is done by the Government. The best shops only accept dollars, they usually do not have any ads or shop windows, and are closed as if they were clandestine, which is not the case.

25

Edecio Bilacha, 67, fought in the '59 revolution on horseback. He was captured by the Batista forces and today works for the Revolution Defense Committee, which supervises the quarters of Havana and of Cuba.

18

Ernesto Baillaro, 70, married, one daughter and three grandchildren. He used to be a refrigeration mechanic but now is a chef in one of the city's many restaurants. The stuffed turtle is his lucky charm.

21

Manuel, 45, earns five dollars a day with his rickshaw taxi. His father is also a taxi driver.

27

Dayne Ribas, 19, an orphan, lives with her brother and is studying economics. At night she seeks amusement at the tourist night clubs. The convertible Buick 58 belongs to a friend.

29

Barbara Garcia, 30, housewife (sitting on the TV set) and her sisters Maria de Los Angeles Garcia, 31, pedagogy assistant and Nancy Garcia, 25 and Carlos Garcia, 3, live together in one of the *solares habaneros*, an old mansion transformed into a collective dwelling. Only Nancy works - as a cleaning lady in a home. Like most people in Cuba they own their apartment.

35

Manoel Fernandez, 78, an ex-dry cleaner. Maria Zandin, 71, ex-fashion designer and her grand daughter Zoila Josefa of 28. Zoila works in a retirement home and her husband is a sailor. Son Alejandro Alberto, 10, (in the background) wants to become a baseball player. The chickens, reared in cages, are for their own consumption.

41

Roberto Denis Morehon, 44. Lasy Diana Gomes, 34. Maria Ester, 14. Margelis (in the mirror), 9. Roberto is unemployed, bakes pizzas at home to sell in the streets for one dollar each. Bruno the pig, reared in the apartment, is an investment: once he is good and fat he'll be sold in pieces. Bruno's vocal chords have been cut so he won't bother the neighbors.

31

Ana Maria Sapeña, 21. To get married in the Palácio de Matrimônio one has to make a reservation one year in advance. The State provides the trousseau - one pair of panties, one pair of underpants, one sheet and two towels - and promises a 3-day honeymoon in some hotel in Cuba. Meals are separate. Rental for a bridal gown costs 120 Cuban pesos (roughly six dollars).

36

Pedro Quintana, 68, three children, two grand children. He used to be a construction worker and today receives a pension, but lives by working as a sweeper in the streets of Havana.

43

Upon retiring, the elderly have the right to free accommodation from the State. Even so, the majority depend upon family members in Miami to be able to buy medicines.

32/33

Giraldilla Group of African Dancing, rehearse in the Casa de Cultura. Art and culture in Cuba, a country with a strong African influence, are encouraged by the State.

39

Rosa Borges, 6. Her father is a mechanic and her mother a nurse.

44

Juan Ricardo Allende, 20, an electronic engineering student. The son of an army major, a hero in Angola. Privileged, they live in a four bedroom apartment in one of the best buildings in Old Havana, with a colour TV set and sound system. He likes swimming, discos, and dreams of working with computers.

46/47

52/53

59

Ana Iris, 24, five brothers, lives with her husband and one daughter, She hopes to join a tourism school. "Tourism's the most beautiful profession" she says "and it's where the dollars are".

Unable to import spare parts due to the American blockade, Cubans are among the most creative mechanics in the world.

Free medical service is a priority in Cuba and includes the right to every type of treatment in public clinics. Doctors however are poorly paid and there are not enough medicines to go around.

49

55

60

With no other toys, Cuban children play with gas masks and equipment left over from the civil war in Angola.

To arrive at their school at 7:30 pm, these young dancers have to leave their homes at 4:30 pm. If the transport system worked better the girls would make the trip in less than twenty minutes.

Influenced by foreign magazines that fall into her hands, she dreams, at 20, of becoming a fashion model. She sees her only chance as being "abroad", on the other side of the sea separating Cuba from America.

50

57

63

Joel Muir, six. His father is a baker and his mother a housewife. He wants to be a car mechanic when he grows up.

A fifth grade student, already worried about his future profession, as in Cuba a tyre repair man working free lance earns five times as much as an engineer, who is obliged to work for the Government.

Luis Henrique Carrion, 28, single, lives with his sisters. He was a judo fighter, but a heart operation when he was 18 put an end to his career. He dreams of leaving Cuba and moving to another country. He says he loves to travel but has never had the opportunity.

64/65

71

76/77

In Cuba all children have access to schools all day, where they are fed and take a nap in the afternoons.
"By practicing on a smaller table" jokes a Cuban Ping-Pong player, "when we play in a championship we always win".

Part of a salsa band, these musicians play in tourist night clubs charging ten dollars entrance fee, far beyond the pockets of most Cubans, who earn that much in a month.

The majority of the buildings in Old Havana either have no running water, have no water pump or it is broken, or else there is no electricity. The daily routine is to go to the water truck, fill a container and take it home, often in buildings with no elevator.

66

72

78

"Climbing the stairs with a bicycle is nothing", says a Cuban who prefers to remain anonymous. "The hard part is having no money to properly feed my family. "

José Calvo, 70. "To dress well when the rest of the world is falling apart always helps" he says, adding "At least psychologically I'm a success".

Young bricklayer at work restoring the buildings of Old Havana, the majority deteriorating from time and neglect.

69

75

81

Marco Martinez, 33, married, one son. He is an amateur weight lifter and works on a fishing boat. In Cuba physical culture is not recognized as a sport by the Government. Martinez works out in clandestine academies and was elected Mr. Cuba in 1989. The idol of the weight lifters is an almost unknown Cuban, exiled and living in Miami, who became Mister Universe.

Lázaro Valdez, 41, three children. A construction worker. As a form of protest he tattooed a picture of the Virgin Mary on his chest, using a sewing needle and ink.

Giovanni Sanches, 20, works in civil construction and plays football (soccer).

83

Geraldo Rubem Gonzalez Dias, 56, is the janitor of the building he lives in and earns his living from a warehouse on the ground floor. A *santero* for 29 years – his grandmother was also a *santera* – he is a "son" of *Iemanjá*. In mystic Cuba, Iemanjá, the black Virgin, is much worshipped. Cults with animal sacrifices are allowed if authorized in advance by the Government.

88/89

Anai Contreras, 21, single, is a landscape painter. Her father works in the food brigade, responsible for bringing food to Havana. Her mother is supervisor in the tourism department of the Banco Nacional.

94/95

Reynaldo Martinez, 35, married, two children. A second *dan* in karate, he works as a guard in the Palácio de los Capitanes Generales, the extreme of Cuban baroque design, built in 1776, today housing the Museu de La Ciudad.

84

Lilian Ávila Figuela, 16, pedagogy assistant. Her father escaped to Miami and sends money every month to her and to her mother. She wants to study legal medicine to study death and the dead.

91

Ana Gloria Garcia, 25, married, two children. She is a primary school teacher and her husband a curator of art works, two privileged professions in Cuba.

97

René Riyes, 38, two children. A butcher, he says "I'm a butcher but there's no meat".

87

Ramon Soares, 26, married, one daughter. He sells almost 300 kilos of grapefruit daily in one of the state fruit stores. Each day he is given one single fruit in season, as well as a wild orange, a lemon and a common orange. By Western standards these fruits are incredibly cheap.

92

Elena de Arras, 28, divorced, with one daughter, is a barmaid. Her previous employment had been as secretary in the Havana College of Economics.

98

Faustino Soret, 88, two children, eight grand children. A retired baseball player, he was a cowboy until he came to Havana in 1919. He fought in the Cuban revolution.

100

Sergio Santa Cruz, 60. A barber, he cuts up to twenty haircuts per day, charging 1 peso cubano (5 cents of a dollar) for a shave and 2 pesos (10 cents) for a haircut. He used to be a stevedore at the docks. "I make much more as a free lance barber" he says.

107

Laura Dias Gomes, 34, divorced, one 19 year-old daughter. She has been a professional dancer for 15 years, and her group, like many others, is supported by the Government.

113

Manoel Solana, 73, divorced, one son and three grandchildren. He is a journalist and a radio announcer. For ten years he worked for the Hotel Nacional in Havana in the summer, and while it was still possible, looked after a hotel in Miami during winter. As a pensioner, he receives 120 pesos cubanos (6 dollars).

103

Miriam Vega, 30, lives with her parents, her husband, two sisters and a niece. She is a civil engineer, worked for some time in the field, but gave up due to the bad conditions. Today she is an employee in the Museu do México.

108/109

The Government also supports several African folklore dancing groups who circulate through the streets of Old Havana.

115

Lali Pereira, 26, single, one six-year-old son. She handcrafts maracas which she sells to tourists in the Plaza de la Catedral square.

104

Arquimedes Hernandez, 55, three children, has been a taxi driver for 25 years, now drives a taxi for the Government, for which he pays 106 pesos cubanos (5 dollars) rental per day. He sometimes earns no more than 10 pesos cubanos (50 cents of a dollar) per day. "It's a living", he says. Private taxis, usually illegal, make up to 50 dollars per day.

110

Humberto Broche, 54, married, two children. His home, in the heart of Habana Vieja where he has lived for 45 years, is the oldest in the neighborhood. He is a technical electrician but works for the State education. His son is the manager of a hotel, his wife, a comedy theater receptionist, while his daughter (in the photo) wants to be a painter.

116/117

With the economic changes, street markets have proliferated. The most traditional one is in the Plaza de la Catedral square, in the heart of Old Havana, where Cubans earn a few dollars posing with the tourists.

119

Ramon Espinoza, 10, is in the fifth grade. His father is a truck mechanic and his mother works in a ticket booth at the railway station. He has two brothers who live in Miami and sometimes send clothes, shoes and toys to their family in Havana.

124

Ana Grehuet, 31, as a manicurist earns more polishing nails than does a doctor of medicine. Lourdes Ivangue Socer (on the stairs) is 20. She is unemployed and wants to learn her friend's profession to find work.

130

Coralina Rodrigues, 35, divorced, one daughter, is an actress in the Grupo de Teatro de Arte Folclorico. Here she poses in front of the headquarters of the Cuban communist party.

120

Victor Rafael Torres, 10 months old, with his grandmother's stuffed alligator.

126/127

Juan Pebonó, 12. His father is a sailor, and he dreams of becoming a naval engineer.

133

Juan Miguel, 26, married, one son, earns eight pesos cubanos per day working for the Municipal Government. His wife works as a cleaner in the port.

123

Rodolfo, 34. Fé, 29, and Rodolfito. Married for two years, as they have no home of their own, they cannot live together. She lives with her mother, cousins and aunts; he sleeps in the family room with an aunt. Rodolfo is a driver at an electricity plant, Fé is head of the financial department in a branch of the Banco Nacional de Cuba.

129

"Cuba has the largest number of doctors per inhabitant in Latin America" claims the doctor. "The problem is that we are very poorly paid (roughly twenty dollars per month) and there is a lack of medicines due to the American blockade."

135

Sahyli (Sali) Toscano, 17, is a classic ballet dancer, having studied since she was 5 years old. She came to Havana from the city of Santo Espiritu, where her father is Chief of Culture and her mother director of a museum. She lives alone with her dog Chester.

Sponsored by

SOCIALCHEQUE
Refeição - Alimentação - Transporte

Supported by

SECRETARIA DE CULTURA DO
ESTADO DE SÃO PAULO

FRIOZEM

LABTEC

Apoio Institucional
Prefeitura Municipal de São Paulo
Lei nº 10.923/90

Printed in Italy

DBA® Dórea Books and Art
Al. Franca, 1185  cj 31/32  Cerqueira César
zip code 01422 010  São Paulo  SP  Brazil  Phonefax (5511) 852 1643  280 3361